THE CHILDREN'S BOOK
OF HEROINES

JEANNE SET OUT TO ATTACK MARGNY

Charles E. Buchel

THE CHILDREN'S
BOOK OF HEROINES

By
F. H. LEE

Illustrated by
HONOR C. APPLETON

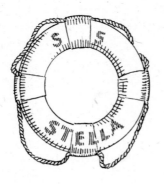

GEORGE G. Harrap & CO. LTD.
LONDON   TORONTO   BOMBAY   SYDNEY

First published 1940
by GEORGE G. HARRAP & CO. LTD.
182 *High Holborn, London, W.C.*1

Made in Great Britain. Printed by Jarrold & Sons, Limited
Norwich

CONTENTS

I

A Daring Rescue

On September 5, 1838, the steamship *Forfarshire* set out from Hull for Dundee. Even in calm weather the ship was hardly fit for the voyage, for her boilers were leaky, so it is no wonder that when a strong gale arose, her engines were quickly flooded and became quite useless.

As the storm increased, the ship was tossed helplessly about and driven before the wind. The crew tried to use her sails, but no sooner were these unfurled than they were torn to shreds.

At the mercy of the waves, the *Forfarshire* drifted near the dangerous coast of Northumberland, and at four o'clock on the morning of September 7 she struck the Harker's Rock, and broke in two.

One part sank rapidly, and with it forty-three people were drowned. Nine others managed to scramble into a boat and were picked up later, out at sea, by another vessel.

The rest, eight men and one woman, were left clinging to the wreck on the rock with little hope of being rescued. For two hours the poor woman struggled to keep her two children alive, but they died in her arms. The heavy seas threatened many times to sweep them all into the sea. Their position was desperate.

About half a mile away was the Longstone Lighthouse, built on one of the Farne Islands; and there the keeper, William Darling, had spent an anxious night, for the waves were mountainous high, and

EVEN IN CALM WEATHER THE SHIP WAS HARDLY FIT
FOR THE VOYAGE

again and again he had scanned the sea for the sight of any ships in distress.

About a quarter to five in the morning, with a gale still blowing from the north, he and Grace, his twenty-two-year-old daughter, set about securing things out of doors, when Grace saw through the telescope that there was a boat on Harker's Rock. But, because of the darkness and the spray, she could not tell whether there were people on board.

By seven o'clock the tide had gone down a little, and she then saw clearly several figures on the rock. The brave girl at once determined to try and save them, and, calling her father, she begged him to set out in their boat.

At first he refused, saying it was madness to try

THEY HAD A MILE TO ROW

even to launch the boat, and if they ever reached the wreck, the heavy seas and strong current would prevent their being able to return to the lighthouse.

But Grace pleaded so earnestly that at last he consented. Mrs Darling helped to launch the boat, and then went to the lighthouse-tower to keep watch.

They had a mile to row, and again and again they were hidden from sight for a long while by the raging billows. It seemed certain death for two persons to battle with such seas. Once Mrs Darling fainted, yet hope revived in her heart as she afterwards caught sight of the little boat again, on the crest of a wave.

9

Could their strength hold out? Bravely they toiled on, and at last reached the rock and found the eight men and one woman clinging to the wreck. It was impossible to take them all into the boat, and Mr Darling managed to persuade four of the men to wait till he should return for them.

THEY REACHED THE LONGSTONE

So with four men and the woman, Grace and her father returned to the lighthouse, two of the rescued men helping to row. It was with grateful hearts that they reached the Longstone, where Mrs Darling was ready to help them.

Two of the men went back to the wreck with Mr Darling, and so the other four men were rescued.

When the story of Grace Darling's and her father's wonderful deed became known, honours and gifts were heaped upon them.

People everywhere praised her bravery and proclaimed her a heroine, yet in the midst of it all she remained humble and unspoiled.

She used to say, "I had very little thought of anything but to help them. The sight was so dreadful that I can still imagine I see the sea flying over the vessel."

It is sad to think that Grace Darling only lived a few years after this. A distressing cough began to trouble her; her strength grew less; and she who had battled against the fury of the wind and wave, and given to the utmost of her strength to save others, soon lay helplessly ill.

All the loving care and attention were in vain, and in 1842, when she was only twenty-six years old, her brave life ended. It seemed fitting that she should be buried within sight of the lighthouse where she had lived, and from which she had so nobly risked her life.

II

The Heroic Little Mother

In a lonely cottage among the mountains of West-
morland, a few miles from the lovely green valley
and lake of Grasmere, lived a farmer, Mr Green,
with his wife and six little children.

One winter day in 1807 Mr and Mrs Green had
to go to a farmhouse about six miles away, and were
compelled to leave the cottage and the little ones
in charge of Agnes, the eldest child, who herself was
only nine years old.

There was no other house nearer than Grasmere,
but Agnes was not afraid. She was a sensible little
girl, and all went well till towards evening, when
a snowstorm came on. The hours passed by, and
the children watched anxiously for their father and
mother to return.

Agnes gave the others their supper of porridge
and milk, and they sat together round the peat fire,
which burned on the hearth. Still no one came, and
a great fear fell upon the little family.

At last Agnes put the two youngest, who were
twins, to bed in their cradle, and the others, two
boys and a girl, cuddled near to Agnes again by
the fire and listened. Not a sound was to be heard,
and they grew very lonely. Outside the snow fell
more thickly than ever, and as twelve o'clock struck,

The Heroic Little Mother

Agnes said they must go to bed. She heard them say their prayers, and they all lay down to sleep.

Next morning there were still no signs of the parents, but Agnes did not lose heart, thinking they must have taken shelter somewhere for the night.

SHE TOOK IN A FEW POTATOES

So she busied herself about the work of the cottage. She dressed the little ones, wound up the clock, boiled the milk to prevent it from turning sour, made more porridge, and tidied up the room.

Finding very little food left, she said that all except the youngest must go on short rations. She then made her way through the snow to the peat-stack, and, with the help of the two boys, she pulled down as much peat as she could, and carried it indoors for the fire. She also took in a few potatoes, just enough for one meal.

After dinner she tried to milk the cow, but the poor creature had had no food, and therefore could give but little milk. So Agnes scrambled into the loft and began to pull down some hay for the cow to eat. Her poor little body was very weary, but she toiled on bravely, hoping every moment to hear the voices of her father and mother.

She wanted to go to Grasmere to ask news of them, but the snow was too deep, and the rather tumble-down bridge over the stream was hidden beneath the snow and was too dangerous to cross.

So the day passed by, and when supper-time came, she undressed the twins and sang them to sleep. Then, as before, the other children cuddled together round the peat fire.

Again midnight struck and once more the brave little family went to bed, only to find the snow still falling in the morning.

The third lonely day went by, and Agnes made the children say their prayers many times. It was hard work to keep them at all cheerful, and once again the little mother put the twins to bed and waited. She tried to keep back her tears, but she was losing heart. If only the snow would stop, she might venture out for help.

The following morning the wind had changed. The snow had ceased and was melting fast. After dressing the children and giving them their break-fast, she decided to make her way to Grasmere.

The two little boys came with her as far as the top of the hill, but she knew the journey would be too long and too unsafe for them, so she sent them home again and trudged on alone.

At last she reached Grasmere and knocked at the door of the first house there. When she asked for

SHE TRUDGED ON ALONE

news of her father and mother, and told of her three lonely days snowed up in the cottage, the people were alarmed.

Parties of men were at once formed, and all pathways of the mountains around were searched, but in vain. There were no traces of the father and mother. Meantime help was sent to the little family among the hills.

At length, after three days, the search-parties, aided by clever dogs, found the bodies of Mr and

Mrs Green quite dead. Mrs Green was wearing her husband's coat and lay near the edge of a cliff, while Mr Green's body was found at the bottom of the rocks down which he had fallen. In the mist and snow they must have wandered far from the pathway and become hopelessly lost.

This was sad news to bring to the brave little maid waiting so anxiously in the cottage, but kindly friends were ready to help. Good homes were found for all the children among the farm-folk near Grasmere, and the sister of the poet Wordsworth became their great friend.

When Queen Charlotte heard of the little heroine of the cottage, she, together with many other people, sent splendid gifts, so that the children's lives might be made happy, even though they had lost the loving care of their own parents.

III

The Heroine of Calabar

NEARLY a hundred years ago there lived in Scotland a little factory-girl. She was the eldest of seven children, and she started work in the mills when only seven years of age.

Her father was a shoemaker, but his drunken and evil ways kept the home very poor, and the mother, having hard work to bring up her family, was very glad of all the help Mary could give.

Mary had little time to learn, but she used to read while at work, propping her book up on the machines. On Sundays she gathered together some of the rough boys of Dundee and so carried on her own little Sunday school.

But she longed most of all to go as a missionary to Calabar on the west coast of Africa, and though she knew it was called the White Man's Grave, yet this only made her all the more eager, and in 1876, two years after Livingstone's death, Mary set sail.

On arriving in Africa she had to journey through dark and unhealthy forests where travelling was difficult. Often the only way was by canoe; the storms and torrential rain were terrifying to her; and the natives seemed given up to every kind of evil and savage cruelty.

They lived in fear of the witch-doctor, who was all-powerful and often ordered human sacrifices to be given to alligators and other creatures, saying these were dragons and needed human blood. Human skulls too were set up as idols, and innocent people were frequently tortured with fire.

SHE DARED TO RESCUE LITTLE TWIN BABIES

If twins were born, the mother was thought to be possessed by evil spirits and was turned out to die of starvation in the forest, while the babies were brutally killed and their bodies eaten by wild animals.

Into the midst of people such as these, Mary Slessor came, fearlessly preaching and teaching, with no thought of her own safety. When she dared to rescue little twin babies and befriend their mother, the witch-doctors said evil would come to the whole tribe. But Mary was not afraid, and soon the natives began to understand her way of love.

Everywhere she went she seemed able to win the hearts of the natives and turn them to better things. She travelled where no white person had ever been, and was called 'Ma' by all the tribes.

Once a chief sent his own state canoe to bring her to his camp, and when she arrived crowds of natives gathered round just to touch her, and watch her eat, and hear her talk.

She tried to preach to them and to help them in other ways. She showed them how to wash and iron and do needlework, and taught them more healthy habits. She had no fear, and even dared to reprove the chief himself for flogging his slaves so cruelly. So great indeed was her power that in a short time he began to treat them more kindly.

On her return journey a terrible storm arose, and the boat was nearly wrecked. Mary had to sit for hours in water up to her knees. This brought on a fever, and for months she was very ill.

After being in Africa for six years, she was ordered to England to rest, but before three years had gone she was out in Africa again, determined to go farther than ever inland.

"I am going to a new tribe," she said, "a fierce, cruel people. Every one says they will kill me, but I don't fear any hurt."

She went by canoe, taking with her five little

orphan children that she had rescued from death. On landing, they had to walk through the dripping forest, their clothes soaked and their feet slipping in the black mud.

Mary, "the White Mother," carried the baby girl, and though she sang to keep the children

SHE WAS IN TRUTH WEARIED OUT

cheerful, she was in truth wearied out and very near tears herself. On arriving at the village, the natives were away feasting at a distance, so Mary had to make a second journey to the canoe for food and clothing, and when the villagers returned, she lay with bleeding feet and scarcely able to move. Yet the very next day she preached to them, and then set to work to make a little home for herself and the orphans.

The natives were slow to help. At first they just

watched her day by day as she built up her strange little house.

Their habits were dirty, and many of their ways were evil, but she taught them patiently, and gradually they learned to be better, even beginning to help her build a church.

They were most interested in her clock, her sewing-machine, her looking-glass, her dishes, and her curtains. These they wanted to have for their own.

When she tried to help them carry on trade, she found that no trader dare come near this fierce tribe, so Mary herself set out in a boat with a store of yams, oil, and spices, and in time she made more trade possible. She taught the people also to improve their own huts and their village, and they started to cut down trees and till the ground.

Afterwards she became a kind of magistrate or governor among the tribes, and they would come to her to decide their quarrels. One day many chiefs arrived, each guarded by twenty to fifty armed men.

They seated themselves, each under a huge umbrella, and Mary had her chair placed in the middle, hardly knowing whether they would be friendly to her or not.

Taking out her knitting, she worked away, listening to first one and then another. Hour after hour the palaver went on and, last of all, they asked her to speak. She told them what they ought to do, and to her surprise, they meekly agreed to do as she had said, and the palaver was over.

Mary returned home very tired, but strangely moved by her power over these ignorant, childlike, yet quarrelsome people. She, who had at one time been only a little factory-girl, had by God's help changed thousands of lives, and about fifty churches and schools were begun as a result of her work in Calabar.

Soon the Government officials heard of all she had 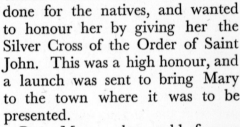 done for the natives, and wanted to honour her by giving her the Silver Cross of the Order of Saint John. This was a high honour, and a launch was sent to bring Mary to the town where it was to be presented.

Poor Mary, who could face a whole gathering of chiefs and natives, was very ill at ease among the grand Government officers. Her old straw hat and cotton dress and slippers looked strangely out of place. She was the heroine of the hour, but, as she sat on the platform, she buried her face in her hands, and when asked to speak she said, "Who am I that I should have this? If I have done anything in my life it has been because my Master has gone before me."

So back once more Mary went to her work, journeying to still more distant villages. She seemed to have a charmed life, and her faith in God and the people never faltered.

The Heroine of Calabar

She worked unceasingly, and everywhere she led the natives to a better way of life. At last, in 1915, when sixty-six years old, she was taken ill with fever, and in a few weeks the heroine of Calabar lay down her life among those she had so nobly loved and served.

IV

The Friend of Prisoners

MR AND MRS GURNEY and their large family lived
in a lovely country house near Norwich called
Earlham Hall. The children had a very happy life,
for their father was a rich banker and could afford
to give them many joys. They loved to ride and
sing and dance and dress gaily.

On Sundays they were taken to the little Quaker
meeting-house at Norwich, though the children did
not altogether like this bare building, and the service
held there seemed to them very unattractive.

One of the girls called Elizabeth was not very
fond of lessons and she had rather a poor opinion
of herself, for her sisters seemed so much cleverer
than she was. When young, too, she had a great
fear of the dark and used to dream often of guns
and being shipwrecked, though her sisters laughed
at her for this.

In 1795, when she was fifteen years old, she was
taken to Norwich to a building called Bridewell. It
was a House of Correction, where women who had
done wrong were kept. For a long while afterwards
she could not forget the misery she saw there, and
then she began to grow very serious. She gave up
many of her joys, dressed less gaily, and spent much
of her time visiting sick people.

The Friend of Prisoners

She began a school for poor children. This she managed all by herself, even when there were seventy scholars. Though her sisters teased her she paid no heed. She dressed always in the quiet grey of the

VISITING SICK PEOPLE

Quakers, and spent her time in loving care for others.

When she was twenty years old she married Joseph Fry. They lived at first in London, where she still carried on her work among the poor. Then to her great joy, they moved to the country, and though she herself had twelve children, she always seemed to find time to help others.

One day in 1813 she went to London, and while she was there she paid a visit to Newgate Prison. She was horrified at the miseries the prisoners had

SHE WAS HORRIFIED

to suffer. They were crowded together in dirty, dark rooms, and many children had even been born there.

The women washed, cooked, and slept on the floor. Many were half naked, and many died of hunger. If the prisoners had money they could have a fire, but few could afford this. They spent their time in evil ways and were treated with great cruelty.

The Friend of Prisoners

When visitors came to the prison the women, who were behind iron bars, used to thrust out large wooden spoons tied to the end of sticks and beg for money or food. They would fight among themselves like animals in the struggle to get help from visitors.

When Elizabeth Fry and her friends entered, the keeper said they had better take off their watches, lest the women snatched at them, but Elizabeth refused. She gave food and clothing to the women and spoke kindly to the prisoners, who were so amazed at being treated thus that a hush stole over them all. Then, kneeling down before Elizabeth and her friends, they begged them to come again.

Next time she went, Elizabeth asked the keeper to leave her alone with the prisoners, but he warned her that this was most unwise, for they were dangerous people. She insisted on being left, however, and the keeper went out, very unwillingly.

Elizabeth then gave them the food and clothes she had brought and afterwards read to them a parable from the Bible. They listened quietly and were very thoughtful.

This was the beginning of many visits to Newgate, and the women looked forward eagerly to her coming. Gradually they forgot their evil ways and grew clean and tidy and kindly.

She collected money to give them little comforts, and taught them how to make clothes for themselves and then for other prisoners too. She even started a school for the children in one of the cells.

Soon her work became known to members of Parliament. She was asked questions about it, and she pleaded strongly for more space, better food, and fairer treatment for the prisoners.

She visited other prisons up and down the land

THE WOMEN LOOKED FORWARD EAGERLY
TO HER COMING

and found them all in a terrible state. In some prisoners were chained to the floor or wall or the bed, and there were hundreds of people ill with gaol-fever.

Yet everywhere she went she helped to put fresh heart into the prisoners, and gradually, because of her work, better laws were passed by Parliament.

Before long, however, her own health gave way,

and she was ordered a long rest. Yet she could not forget her work, and as she grew stronger, she visited ports from which convict-ships set out, five and six times a year, for Australia.

There she found women chained together, many carrying babies in their arms. She learned that on the terrible journey of nearly a year, prisoners often became insane, food was scarce, and many perished with the cold.

Year after year Elizabeth struggled on against these evils and did not give up till matters were improved.

Kings and great people in many lands helped and honoured her, but the strain of the work on her health proved too great, and she grew weaker, till on October 12, 1845, this brave woman died, having spent her life in the service of the helpless and oppressed.

V

Her Father's Pardon

MORE than a hundred years ago a Russian officer, Captain Lopouloff, who had offended the Tsar, was banished with other exiles to Siberia, a terribly cold and dreary land. His life there was one of great hardship, and he grieved very much that his wife and little daughter, Prascovia, about three years old, had to endure such suffering with him.

Many times he sent letters to ask for another trial or for a pardon, but it was in vain and, as Prascovia grew older, she had to find work in the village or in the fields.

At first she was happy enough, never having known any better life, but gradually she began to understand why her father was so troubled, and she prayed each day that in some way he might be made more cheerful.

One day, when she was saying her prayers, it flashed into her mind that she herself might go to the Tsar at Saint Petersburg and beg for her father's pardon.

She dared not tell her parents of her wish at first, but she did not cease to pray about it, and one day she took courage and asked her father if she could go. He smiled, as if amused by such a strange request, and said jokingly to his wife, "My wife, good news, our daughter is going off to Saint Petersburg to speak for us to the Emperor."

"She ought to be attending to her work instead of talking nonsense," she replied.

Poor Prascovia wept because they refused to take

SHE PRAYED EACH DAY

her seriously, and for three years her life went on as usual. Yet she never gave up hope, and having nursed her mother through a severe illness, she persuaded them to listen to her once more.

Still, however, they tried to prevent her, saying it was too dangerous a journey and that she had no passport for travelling. But she got a friend to write for one, and in six months it arrived.

Her father now became angry with her and locked the passport away, yet still she persevered, and at last he said to his wife, "We shall have to let this child go. Yet how can she hope to see the Emperor. Sentinels guard every entrance, and they will never let a beggar pass inside."

At length, on September 8, she was allowed to start. Kneeling before her parents, she received their blessing, and, with only one rouble in her pocket, she began her long, long journey.

The first night she spent at a friend's house, and then went on alone. It seems impossible that a girl of nineteen should have had courage to face the difficulties of such a journey.

SHE WENT ON ALONE

Often she lost her way; many times she was roughly treated; sometimes she slept in woods; and at others she was soaked to the skin by storms.

Once she tried to take shelter in a church, but the doors were locked, and, as she sat on the stone steps, the village boys hooted at her and called her a thief and a runaway. Her feet became swollen and blistered, yet on she trudged, trusting that God would help her.

At some places, in return for her food, she worked for the people, doing washing or sweeping or sewing.

Then winter began to set in, and for eight days a snowstorm forced her to stop. Some kindly drivers, however, offered her a seat in their sledge. She was very glad of this, but her clothes were so poor that she was nearly frozen with the cold and had to be lifted from the sledge at night. Next day the drivers lent her one of their fur coats, each taking it in turns to go without.

Then a lady called Madam Milin took care of her for a while. She gave her money and got her a place on a barge going towards St Petersburg. While on the barge she was accidentally thrown into the river and, though rescued, had to stay in her wet clothes. This brought on a serious illness, and she would have died had not some friendly nuns nursed her till she was strong enough to travel by sledges to St Petersburg.

She was overjoyed at reaching the city at last, eighteen months after she had left home. For the next fortnight she took her stand each day upon the steps of the Senate House, holding out her petition to anyone who looked like a senator. But no one noticed her, and she was almost giving up in despair when a lady, touched by her story, offered to take her to the Tsar's mother.

THE DRIVERS LENT HER ONE OF THEIR FUR COATS

With trembling heart she set out, and when she reached the palace she said, "Oh, if my father could see me now, how glad he would be. My God, finish Thy work!"

The Empress-mother received her kindly. She listened to her story, praising her for her courage and her love for her father, and, having given her three hundred roubles, she said she would speak for

34

her to the Tsar. To poor Prascovia it seemed too good to be true, and she wept for very gladness.

Two days later she was taken to the Tsar, who gave her five thousand roubles and promised to attend to her petition.

Then came the joyous news that her father's pardon was granted, and the Emperor bade her also say what she wished to have as a present for herself.

She wanted nothing for herself, however, and asked that two other of her father's friends might also be pardoned. The Emperor, moved by her unselfishness, granted her request, and she set out towards home with a heart full of gratitude.

Her father and mother scarcely knew what to say when they saw their heroic daughter, and kneeling before her, would have humbled themselves in her presence, but she cried out, herself kneeling, "What are you doing? It is God, God only who works for us."

One glad week they spent together; then her parents journeyed back to their own home, while Prascovia went to live with the nuns who had befriended her.

A great gladness and peace filled her life, but her health had been shattered by the hardship and sufferings of her journey, and on the morning of December 9, 1809, the nuns found that her brave soul had passed on to God, in whom she had trusted and who had so truly helped her.

VI

Her Life for Her Country

EDITH CAVELL was born in the year 1866. Her father was vicar of Swardeston, in Norfolk, and little did her parents dream that this baby girl would one day sacrifice her life for her countrymen.

She was bright, and loved games, but she was unusually thoughtful for a child and never happier than when she was helping other people. It was natural, then, that, as she grew older, she wanted to be a nurse, and she went for her training to the London Hospital.

Afterwards she worked in other hospitals, and everywhere she proved herself very skilful.

She put duty before everything else and expected others to do the same. She hated younger nurses under her charge to be careless about their work.

In 1906 she went to Brussels to help to improve the hospitals and nursing-homes there, and she also started a training-school for nurses.

While she was on holiday in Norwich in August, 1914, war was declared between Germany and England, and the Germans began to march through Belgium.

Nurse Cavell at once decided to return to her hospital, saying, "I must be over there. I shall be wanted." On arriving she found that German troops were already firing on the city, and by August 20 they were actually marching beneath her hospital windows.

It was not long before wounded soldiers were being brought in. There were Germans, French,

WOUNDED SOLDIERS WERE BEING BROUGHT IN

Belgians, and English all needing treatment, and to them all she gave her utmost care. It was natural, however, that she should want to aid her own countrymen and their allies, so she began to supply British, French, and Belgian soldiers with food, clothes, and even money, secretly helping them to escape across the border into Holland, where the Germans had no power.

37

Baron von Bissing, the German general, began to suspect that she was assisting her own countrymen, and spies were therefore set to trap her, while orders were given that no one was to help the enemy soldiers.

For nearly a year she quietly and courageously

SHE SECRETLY HELPED THEM
TO ESCAPE

carried on her work. Then on the evening of August 5, 1915, while attending to the wounded in her hospital, she was arrested by the Germans and taken to St Gilles' prison, where she was thrust into a cell.

For three weeks no one in England knew what had happened, till a chance traveller happened to tell the news. The English leaders at once began to make inquiries, but all their efforts were in vain.

Her Life for Her Country

After being kept a prisoner for two months, she was led from the cell to be tried secretly. Her face was deathly pale, but her spirit was undaunted. She spoke without trembling, and when asked why she had helped soldiers to get to England, she replied,

"If I had not done so, they would have been shot. I thought I was only doing my duty in saving their lives."

She was refused permission to send any letter or message to her friends, and was led back to her cell to wait her sentence. Meantime English and American statesmen and others were doing all in their power to save her from death, but three days later this noble woman was condemned to be shot at dawn.

At eleven o'clock, the night before her death, an English chaplain, Mr Gahan, was allowed to visit her. He found her calm and unafraid.

"I have no fear nor shrinking," she said. "I have seen death so many times that it is not strange or fearful to me." And she added, "I thank God for ten weeks' quiet, for life has always been hurried and full of difficulty. Patriotism is not enough. I must have no hatred or bitterness towards anyone."

She listened calmly as Mr Gahan read through the first verses of the hymn, 'Abide with me,' and she joined in the last verse,

Hold Thou Thy cross before my closing eyes,
Shine through the gloom and point me to the skies,
Heaven's morning breaks and earth's vain shadows flee,
In life, in death, O Lord abide with me.

"Good-bye," she said quietly as the chaplain left her, "we shall meet again."

Early next morning she was led out and, with eyes unbandaged, she stood ready before the soldiers who were to shoot.

Some say they were so moved by her courage that they purposely shot too high and so left her unharmed. Then she fainted and fell to the ground and the officer in charge hurried forward and shot her through the head.

"PATRIOTISM IS NOT ENOUGH"

The German chaplain who was there wrote of her, "She was brave to the last. She died like a heroine."

The hearts of the English people were deeply stirred, and from the King and Queen, as well as from great men and humble folk, came messages of sorrow. On October 29 a solemn memorial service was held in St Paul's Cathedral. It was attended by people of all ranks, as well as by many wounded soldiers, and more than two thousand nurses. The hymn, 'Abide with me,' was sung during the service, and, as the procession moved out, the nurses fell on their knees in honour of their brave comrade.

After some time her body was taken from its

burial-place near the prison of St Gilles, and brought to England. From Dover the funeral-train passed through the beautiful orchards of Kent, then in full bloom. On arriving at Victoria Station, the coffin, draped with the Union Jack, was borne to Westminster Abbey.

Queen Alexandra was present at the service there and sent a wreath of red and white carnations and arum lilies. On the card, which was attached, she had written:

> Life's race well run,
> Life's work well done,
> Life's crown well won,
> Now comes rest.

After the service the coffin was taken to Norwich, where, in a quiet corner of the cathedral grounds called 'Life's Green,' Nurse Cavell's body was laid to rest near the grave of her own mother.

She had given her life for her country, and later a statue was erected in her honour near the National Gallery. On it are engraved the words she spoke so shortly before her death:

Patriotism is not enough. I must have no hatred or bitterness for anyone.

VII

A Humble Heroine

On the day before Good Friday in the year 1899, the steamship *Stella* left Southampton on its way to the Channel Islands. There were about two hundred holiday-makers on board, and all went well for a short time.

Then, unfortunately, a dense fog came on. The captain, however, decided not to turn back, but to keep to his course, and he steered through the gloom.

After several hours, and just before reaching the island, there was a terrible crash—the ship had struck the rocks and almost immediately it began to sink.

Orders were hurriedly given for life-boats to be lowered and all life-belts to be put on. A stewardess called Mrs Mary Rogers went quickly among the women passengers, helping them to fasten their life-belts and seeing them into the life-boat. Finding one woman without a life-belt, she quietly undid her own and gave it up to her.

At last all those in her care were safely in the life-boat, and the sailors then shouted to the stewardess to take her place in it too.

"No, no," she answered quickly, "one more would sink the boat."

A Humble Heroine

So the life-boat moved off, leaving the brave stewardess on the sinking ship.

"Good-bye, good-bye!" she cried cheerfully, though she knew only too well that in a few moments she herself must be drawn beneath the cruel waves.

Then with uplifted hands, as if in prayer, she waited calmly for the end—a humble but true heroine, for she gave her own life freely that others might be saved.

THE LIFE-BOAT MOVED OFF

VIII

The Brave Maid of France

IN the lovely little French village of Domrémy, on January 6, 1412, Jeanne d'Arc was born. Her father was a farmer, and Jeanne used to help him in his work. She never learned to read or write, but she could sew as well as any lady in the land.

She was very happy playing with her friends, but she loved to steal away to the little church to pray. She often nursed sick folk and many times let poor travellers have her bed, while she lay beside the fire all night.

Every one loved her for her goodness and her simple homely ways, and even birds and animals would feed from her hands.

While quite young she learned that Charles the Dauphin, son of the French king, had been set aside by some of the people, the Burgundians, and was not allowed to be crowned king. The English, too, helped the Burgundians, and the Dauphin had no great leader to fight for him.

One day Jeanne and her friends were running races; she ran so swiftly that her feet scarce seemed to touch the ground, and she easily won the race. As she was resting at the far end of the meadow, some one seemed to appear and told her that her mother needed her. Hastening home, she found that her mother had not called her.

Jeanne was puzzled and was returning to her playmates, when suddenly a bright cloud passed before her eyes, and she heard a voice saying she must change her way of life and do wonderful deeds, for God had chosen her to help the Dauphin. She must therefore wear man's clothes, and take up arms, and be a captain in the war.

"But," said Jeanne, "I am only a peasant girl, and cannot even ride a horse."

The voices came to her so many times that at last she felt she must obey them. She persuaded her cousin to take her to the captain at Vaucouleurs. But he only laughed at her story and said, "Box her ears, and take her back to her father."

Jeanne was not to be turned aside, however, and,

THE VOICES CAME TO HER SO MANY TIMES

after much trouble, she was allowed to set out for Chinon to see the Dauphin.

It was a dangerous journey with poor food and little rest all the time, but Jeanne was always cheerful, saying to her companions, "You must fear nothing, for God has sent me, and to Him all things are possible."

When she reached the castle and was led into the Great Hall, they tried to deceive her by dressing one of the courtiers as the Dauphin. Now she had never seen the Dauphin before, but, guided by her voices, she went straight to the rightful prince, and said, "Most noble Dauphin, I am sent by God to help you. My voices say I have but one year to live. Oh, send me, before it is too late."

Every one was amazed at her words, and, though there were many delays, she was at last given an army. Then, dressed in armour of white steel, over which was a cloak of gold and velvet, and carrying a sword from the altar of St Catherine's Chapel, she rode forth on a jet-black horse.

Her banner was of pure white, embroidered with lilies. On it was a figure of the King of Heaven, bearing the world in his hand. Angels were kneeling beside Him, and below were written the words "Jesus Maria."

"Lead me to Orleans," said Jeanne, "and I will show you a sign, for I will raise the siege and crown the Dauphin."

So to Orleans they came, and there the battle with the English was fierce and long. Yet everywhere the Maid's white banner could be seen as she fought on, cheering her soldiers as she cried, "Doubt not, the place is ours."

Once, when scaling a ladder placed against the

SHE WAS WOUNDED AND FELL

walls, she was wounded and fell, but she was soon back in her place again. The English were amazed at her power, and, thinking she must be a witch, great fear fell on them, and they fled, leaving the peasant girl of seventeen victorious over her enemies.

Other battles followed, but, listening to and obeying her voices, Jeanne triumphed everywhere, and on July 17, to her great joy, the Dauphin was crowned at Rheims Cathedral, while Jeanne stood by his side, her white banner in her hand.

"Gentle king," she said, "now is accomplished the will of God. Let me return to Domrémy."

But the king would not hear of this and bade her stay at the court, where she was treated like a prince, and had a mantle of gold to wear. From the time that she had seen the Dauphin crowned, however, her life became troubled and unhappy, for she longed most of all to drive the English out of France, yet the king preferred a life of luxury and ease to one of struggle, and allowed her few soldiers and little money for any battles.

One April day, while standing on the ramparts of a town she had taken, she seemed to hear her voices very plainly saying, "Before the feast of Saint John, Midsummer Day, you will be taken prisoner, but have no fear, be strong and of good courage, and God will help you."

The brave maid had no fear of death, and she prayed day after day that she might die rather than be long a captive.

Soon afterwards fighting broke out afresh, and one night Jeanne set out with about five hundred men to relieve Compiègne. Suddenly a party of enemy riders appeared. Twice she forced them back, but fresh soldiers came up, and Jeanne's men became alarmed and fled. In the confusion Jeanne was dragged from her horse and captured.

When asked to yield, she held her banner above

her head and cried, "I have given my faith to another than you, and I will keep my oath." That same night she was imprisoned in the castle of Beaulieu.

The French king, Charles, for whom she had risked her life, made no attempt to rescue or ransom her, and seemed to forget all she had done for their land. Yet she remained loyal to Charles and would let no one speak any ill of him.

She tried to escape, but was caught by a gaoler and taken to a fortress forty miles away. While there she leaped down from the battlements of the tower, sixty feet in height. Yet, as if by a miracle, she was not killed, though for two days she was too ill to take food. She had often said she would rather die than fall into the hands of the English, yet before long she was sold to them for six thousand francs, the price of a prince's ransom.

They carried her off to Rouen Castle, where for five months she was chained in a dark cell, by hands, feet, and waist to a heavy log. Even when asleep she was fettered to the bed and suffered both in mind and body.

At the end of February she was led out to be tried as a witch. When brought into the court she wore a page's black suit, her hair cut short to her neck.

The trial lasted six days, and during all that time she was questioned by cruel and clever people, yet her brave spirit never faltered. In every way they tried to trap her, but she was unafraid, saying she had obeyed God and her voices. "If you kill me," she cried, "I will say no other thing. If I were in the fire I would say no more, and till death I will hold that what I have said is truth. I have done nothing against God and the faith."

Soon after she was sentenced to be burned as a witch. For a while she was troubled and wondered

SHE WAS CHAINED IN A DARK CELL

if her voices had led her aright, for all her courage and suffering seemed to have been in vain, but her strength of soul returned, and she faced death as a heroine.

On May 31 her guards led her out to die, arrayed in a long white gown. As she passed through the crowded streets to the market-place, she cried, "Rouen, Rouen, I fear that you will yet suffer because of this."

Slowly she mounted the scaffold. Kneeling down,

she prayed to the Holy Mary and all the Saints and begged forgiveness for her sins. Then, turning to her judges, she said she forgave them all the evil they had done her.

Even her enemies wept to see her. Before being

SHE WAS TROUBLED

bound to the stake, she asked for a cross. There was none to give her, but one of the English soldiers broke his staff into two pieces and tied them together in the shape of a cross. This he gave her, and in joy she clasped it close to her breast.

As the smoke rose she became hidden from sight, but from the midst of the fire her clear strong voice was heard saying, "My voices were of God. They have not deceived me."

Once again the people heard her cry, "Jesus! Jesus!" And, with His name upon her lips, the heroic soul of the Maid of France passed to Heaven.

IX

The Lady of the Lamp

In a beautiful country home in Hampshire lived a little girl called Florence Nightingale. Her life was full of interest amid the fields and trees and flowers and animals and birds, and she and her sister had almost every joy that money could provide.

But as she grew older, Florence longed to be of more use in the world; so she began to visit the cottages round her father's estate, and if any one were ill she would take them little dishes of dainty food. She would help to nurse them too, and she liked this best of all. Her very first patient had been Cap, the shepherd's dog, whose foot was hurt, and she made up her mind to learn more about nursing one day.

Her father and mother little dreamed the thoughts that were passing through her mind, and for some years she led the life of a rich young lady, riding, travelling to other lands, being presented at Court, and mixing with important people.

Yet for none of these things did she really care. Her one desire was to care for the sick. Now at that time, about one hundred years ago, nurses were mostly rough and ignorant people, no lady would think of doing that kind of work. However, Florence at last took courage and asked her mother if she would allow her to go to a hospital to be trained.

Mrs Nightingale could scarcely believe that Florence was serious. Her daughter to leave home and be a nurse! To do unpleasant and dirty work!

HER VERY FIRST PATIENT HAD BEEN CAP,
THE SHEPHERD'S DOG

To touch unhealthy people! Such a thing was impossible, and never would she consent.

So Florence had to give up the idea for the time; but in the end she triumphed, and was allowed to go to hospitals in Germany and Paris, afterwards returning to England. Mrs Nightingale still felt that Florence had disgraced the family, but as the years passed, she began to feel less bitter towards her.

So Florence went on patiently with her task of improving the hospitals in England, and she made people think more highly of a nurse's work than ever before. She even persuaded a few ladies to join her in the hospital.

Then in 1854 war broke out between Russia and England, and many battles were fought in the Crimea. This meant of course that hundreds of soldiers were being wounded. Stories reached England of the terrible suffering of these men. Many were simply left to die, others died because of lack of care and food, and hundreds more were ill with fever.

Florence was so moved by this that she offered at once to go out and take forty nurses with her and care for the wounded. After a terrible voyage of storms and discomfort, they arrived at Scutari, and as they landed they could see the huge barrack-hospital away on a hill.

A rough track led them to it, and as Miss Nightingale went into the various rooms her heart sank within her. It was worse than anything she had imagined.

Hundreds of soldiers lay ill with cholera and fever, many of them too ill ever to recover. The whole place was filthy, scores of rats, both alive and dead, infested the rooms, and many soldiers had to lie crowded on the floor, there being few beds and fewer bedclothes.

The blankets that were there were swarming with fleas, and there were scarcely any bowls or soap or towels for washing, and very little water.

The food was almost entirely boiled meat, dry bread, and very poor tea. It was badly cooked and nearly always cold before the few orderlies could get it to the men, who often had to eat it with their fingers, there being so few spoons or knives or forks.

Bandages and medicine were difficult to obtain. Indeed, it would be hard to imagine anything worse than the state of the hospital when Miss Nightingale entered.

Yet so nobly did she tackle the task, that before many weeks had passed there was a tremendous change. Sisters and nurses made large canvas bags and stuffed them with straw for beds. Mops, scrubbing-brushes, and brooms were bought, many of them paid for by Florence herself. The kitchens were cleaned; the food was more suitable and better cooked; two thousand cotton and flannel shirts were obtained and given out; a laundry was arranged; the soldiers' wounds were properly bandaged; the wards were scrubbed; and so many other improvements were made, that instead of about half the men dying, as before, only about two in every hundred died.

The wounded soldiers on the battlefield thought that if only they could get to the hospital and there find the 'Good Lady' all would be well with them.

Each night Florence, carrying a lamp, would go through all the wards to see that everything possible was being done for the men. This meant a walk of about four miles, after almost every one else had gone to bed, but she never spared herself, however weary she might be.

Her power over the soldiers was wonderful.

Feverish, restless suffering men would feel better just to see her or have a kindly, cheering word from her. Some even used to kiss her shadow as it fell on the wall behind them, and they would wait eagerly every night for the Lady of the Lamp to come.

When the people of England heard of her heroic work, they gave money to help her, and honours were sent from Queen Victoria herself.

Fortunately, in 1856, the war came to an end and the army soon returned home. A warship was sent to bring Florence to England, and a great procession, with massed bands and waving banners, was prepared as a homecoming worthy of this wonderful woman.

But Florence did not wish for fame, and she and

EACH NIGHT FLORENCE, CARRYING A LAMP, WOULD GO THROUGH ALL THE WARDS

her aunt travelled home as private passengers. So, dressed in a plain black cloak and bonnet, the heroine of the Crimea returned quietly to her father's beautiful house at Embley, where she had spent so many happy days, and where now her dearest friends were waiting anxiously to receive her.

As her step sounded on the path, their joy was too great to be told in words. The heart of Florence too was glad, and she was content to rest there awhile. But her work was not yet over, and she was soon busy planning for a school, where nurses could be trained, using the money given her for herself to build it.

The dream of her young life had come true, she had nursed and healed and helped thousands of people, and, best of all, she had made people realize that the work of nursing was a beautiful and noble thing.

PLANNING FOR A SCHOOL

X

The Discovery of Radium

In an almost empty attic in Paris there lived a young Polish girl. She had very little money, her dress was almost threadbare, she was shy and reserved, and scarcely seemed to notice other people at all. Yet life was full of interest to her, for she had travelled from Poland to study science at the Sorbonne, the University of Paris.

Her name was Marie Sklodovska, and she loved her work in the laboratory so much that she grudged every minute spent on other things. She had been a governess in Poland and had been able to save a little money there. This, with small sums given her each month by her father, was all she had, to pay for meals and clothes and for her room and expenses at the University.

She could not afford to go about with her friends, and many times she had to be without a fire till her fingers became numb and her shoulders shook with the cold. Yet she plodded on cheerfully.

She had little money for food, living most of the time on bread and butter and tea. Sometimes, for a special treat, she would buy two eggs or a little fruit or a piece of chocolate. Often she fainted and was ill for lack of food, but still she toiled on with her experiments.

Another young student of science at the University, Pierre Curie, became very interested in Marie. They talked together about their work and grew to love each other, and in less than a year they were married.

They spent their honeymoon roaming round the country on bicycles. They stayed at cheap village

SHE PLODDED ON

inns and lived mostly on bread and cheese and fruit, but they were very happy.

Later on they took a little flat in Paris. There was scarcely any furniture, just two chairs and a white wooden table. These and their books, a lamp and a bunch of flowers were all that they possessed.

Marie would leave a meal to cook itself, while she kept on with her studies, and together they carried on many experiments. The next year a little girl, Irene, was born, and Pierre then took up work as a teacher in a school, while Marie fixed up a rather poor sort of laboratory at home. Here, after caring for her house and baby, she would settle down to her studies.

She was specially interested in a substance called

uranium, which was obtained from pitchblende. Uranium was known to give off very powerful rays by which men could see through many substances; but Marie discovered that what was left after obtaining uranium was even more wonderful and more powerful. Marie determined to find out the secret of these rays, and in a little damp, cold, ground-floor laboratory she began her experiments. Soon Pierre became interested and joined her in her task.

At last they found there must be *two* new substances giving off these rays, though as yet they had not been able to obtain either of them. One they called polonium, in honour of her country Poland, and the other was called radium.

Once more Marie and Pierre set to work, but they were poor and needed a great deal of pitchblende for the experiments. The Government of Austria, however, gave them a ton of it from their mines, and in a little room with no proper floor and with only a few old kitchen-tables and an iron stove, they toiled, overpowered by the heat in summer and frozen with cold in the winter.

"Yet," said Marie in a letter to a friend, "it was in this miserable old shed that the best and happiest years of our life were spent."

Much of the work had to be done in the courtyard, and there Marie Curie might have been seen day after day in a dusty and stained smock, her hair blown by the wind and she herself nearly choked with the bitter smoke, carrying heavy jars, stirring and watching boiling liquids for hours at a stretch.

For four years she struggled against great difficulties, and at last she had produced radium, just a tiny pinch of dull white powder looking something like salt, but it was to become one of the wonders of the world, for its rays could travel one hundred and eighty-six thousand miles a second and one ounce of it would take one hundred thousand years to be used up. With these rays people would be able to see through even the hardest substances. It was two million times stronger than uranium, and only a lead screen could stop its rays. But it needed a whole ton of pitch-blende to produce one ounce of radium.

MUCH OF THE WORK HAD TO BE DONE IN THE COURTYARD

Pierre tested its power on his arm, and it caused burns and a wound that took months to heal. Yet, most wonderful of all, it was found that its rays, if used with care, were able to cure the terrible disease of cancer.

Before long this wonderful discovery became known, though only Marie and Pierre actually knew how to obtain radium. They were asked to banquets and dinners, and honours were heaped upon them. But they did not wish for fame; they wanted only to carry on their work. They refused to *sell* their secret (though in this way they might have become very rich), but nobly *gave* it to the world for the sake of all people.

When a sum of money was given them as a prize, they spent very little on themselves, but gave gifts to others and spent the rest on furthering the work of science.

In 1904 another little girl, Eve, was born, but Marie Curie was soon back at her teaching. Pierre, too, was made a professor at the University, and both worked on so that one day they might build a laboratory worthy of the great cause of science.

Then on April 19 sad trouble came to Marie, for while Pierre was stepping from a pavement he slipped before a heavy wagon, and was dragged along and killed. When Marie heard the news she cried, "Pierre is dead! Dead!"

Her grief was terrible. She clung to his lifeless body and would not be comforted. After the funeral the Government offered her a pension, but she replied, "I want no pension, I am young enough to earn my living."

The University then asked her to carry on Pierre's work as professor, and, despite her sorrow, she set about preparing her first lecture. In the following years she became very famous, and honours were showered upon her in many lands, yet always she was happiest when quietly at work in her own laboratory.

When war was declared in 1914, she fitted out rooms and cars with X-ray apparatus, and more than a million soldiers' wounds were examined in this way.

The building of Institutes of Radium in different places filled Madame Curie's heart with thankfulness, and she had charge of the one in Paris in which thousands of cancer-patients were treated.

She remained comparatively poor, and when asked why she did not make money by her cures, she replied, "I am working for Science. Radium belongs to the people, not to me."

But experiments with radium are dangerous, and many times she did not guard sufficiently against the power of its rays, which, though able to cure some diseases, may also harm those who handle it.

So her hands and arms were burned, her blood became poor, and she was taken ill with fever. In July, 1934, this heroine, who had unselfishly given her own life in the cause of others, was laid to rest beside her husband Pierre, whom she had loved so well, and with whom she had worked so nobly.